DATE			

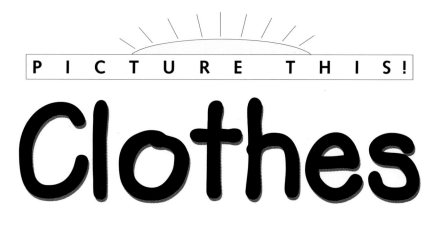

PICTURE THIS!

Clothes

Karen Bryant-Mole

RIGBY
INTERACTIVE
LIBRARY

This edition ©1997 Rigby Education
Published by Rigby Interactive Library,
an imprint of Reed Educational & Professional Publishing
500 Coventry Lane
Crystal Lake, IL 60014

Printed in China
01 00 99 98 97
10 9 8 7 6 5 4 3 2 1

Library of Congress Cataloging-in-Publication Data

Bryant-Mole, Karen.
  Clothes / Karen Bryant-Mole.
    p. cm. — (Picture this!)   Includes index.
  Summary: Text and photographs identify various types of clothing, including that worn on hot and cold days, clothes for sleeping, shoes, hats, and more.
    ISBN 1-57572-149-X (lib. bdg.)
  1. Children's clothing—Juvenile literature.   [1. Clothing and dress.]
  I. Title.   II. Series.
TT635.B79 1997   96-37244
646'.3—dc21   CIP
                                                                       AC

Text designed by Jean Wheeler

Acknowledgments
The publisher would like to thank the following for permission to reproduce photographs:
Tony Stone Images, p. 14 (left); Jerome Tisne, p. 15 (right); Andy Sacks, p. 18 (left and back cover); Jess Stock, (right); Don Spiro, p. 19 (left); David Madison, p. 23 (right); Zigy Kaluzny; (left) Peter Cade/Zefa; p. 14 (right), p. 15 (left), p. 22 (both), p. 23 (right).

Note to the Reader
Some words in this book may be new to you.
You may look them up in the glossary on page 24.

Visit Rigby's Education Station® on the World Wide Web at http://www.rigby.com

Contents

What Clothes Are Made of

Clothes can be made from many different materials.

wool

cotton

plastic

nylon

5

Fabric

Some of the clothes we wear
are made from fabric.

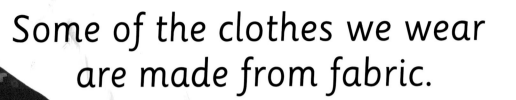

The fabric is cut into pieces using a pattern. The pieces are then stitched together.

Knitting

These clothes have been knitted with yarn.

This sweater has been knitted by machine.

This one
has been
knitted
by hand.

Hot Days

These clothes will keep
you cool on a hot,
sunny day.

sundress

short-sleeved shirt

shorts

11

Cold Days

These clothes will keep you warm on a cold day.

scarf

sweatshirt

socks

heavy pants

13

Nightwear

Some clothes are just for sleeping.

pajamas

sleepers

nightshirt

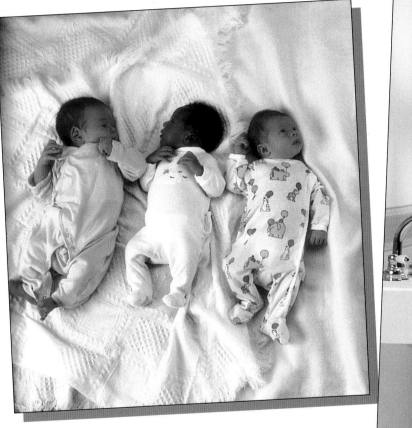

What do you wear at night?

Shoes

rain boots

All of these are worn on your feet.

sneakers

slippers

high tops

sandals

Sports

You need to wear special clothes when you play some sports.

skiing

baseball

karate

soccer

19

Hats

Hats keep you warm and protect you from the sun.

sun hat

ski hat

beach hat

baseball hat

Dressing Up

Dressing up in costumes can be fun.

magician

angel

chef

superhero

Glossary

fabric Type of material, sometimes called cloth. 6

costumes Clothes that make you look like someone else. 22

materials What things are made from. 4

nylon Strong human-made material used to make clothes, rope, brushes, and other things. 5

pattern Model or guide to help make things. 7

stitched Sewn together using a needle and thread. 7

Index

24